A souvenir guide

Dyrham Park and William Blathwayt
Gloucestershire

Rupert Goulding

Hidden Grandeur

Just off the road which takes you into the Cotswolds lies Dyrham Park, a mansion built in the grandest baroque style.

This architectural *tour de force* never fails to strike awe in any visitor who gazes down on it from the top of its sweeping, deer-sprinkled valley. For all its aristocratic splendour, Dyrham was not built by a lord or duke, but by a government and colonial administrator – William Blathwayt (c.1649–1717).

Blathwayt was a curious man, notable for his sustained industry and for his aptitude in dealing with the drudgery of government administration. He lived through a period of turbulence and profound change in British and global history. Born in or around 1649, the year that Charles I was beheaded, William lived through the Commonwealth, the Restoration of Charles II in 1660, the Great Fire of London, and the Glorious Revolution that brought about the reigns of William and Mary. It was a period of great scientific curiosity and economic and geographic expansion, one that left material echoes in the very fabric of Dyrham Park itself.

William inherited the Dyrham estate in 1689 from his father-in-law and immediately set about rebuilding the house, decorating and furnishing it in the Dutch style favoured by the court of William and Mary. At the same time, he laid out ambitious water-gardens to defy the challenging terrain and draw the eye into the landscape.

The end of ambition

Subsequent generations never matched William Blathwayt's dynastic ambition. The gardens, his great indulgence, barely survived his son. Later generations could not or would not maintain them, favouring the more modish parkland of the late Georgian period. The house deteriorated until there came a reprieve in the nineteenth century under Colonel George Blathwayt, who put a stop to the dispersal of Dyrham's contents. Thereafter, much of the twentieth century saw what was in effect a managed decline.

At last Dyrham and its rare preservation came to the attention of the Land Fund, a government body set up in 1946 to secure culturally significant property for the nation; it was purchased as a war memorial to those who had died in the Second World War. Transferred to the National Trust to open in 1961, Dyrham has welcomed visitors ever since to explore and discover this fascinating place, resonant with history.

Opposite **The west front**

Left **The east front**

Above **The Dyrham deer herd**

Servant to Six Monarchs

William Blathwayt was one of the most able government administrators of the late seventeenth century.

Like the famous diarist Samuel Pepys, he combined ability with professionalism; such men heralded what was to become the Civil Service. William's career started in the embassy in The Hague during the reign of Charles II. He found favour and promotion under James II, who was said to hold William in special regard.

When, in 1688, Catholic James was deposed and replaced by Protestant William of Orange and his queen Mary, one might have expected William Blathwayt's career prospects to be scuppered, but his ability to speak Dutch and his natural efficiency soon made him indispensable to the new king. William III was an impatient man, who valued an administrator like William Blathwayt to act as a buffer between the Crown and the sprawling machinery of government. Under Queen Anne, William Blathwayt's many roles started to ebb away, but he remained involved in colonial matters until his death in the reign of George I.

Right **William Blathwayt,** the creator of Dyrham; by Michael Dahl c.1689–91

A man of parts

William's chief appointment was as Surveyor and Auditor General of Plantation Revenues, a long-standing role which led him to become an expert on the British colonies. His task was to audit the royal revenues owed by the colonists, so that they should not be dependent on subsidy from London, but instead become financial contributors to the wealth of the nation. Describing his own legacy, William once wrote that his work made 'desperate ventures of little importance', into 'necessary and important members' of the realm.

He never visited any of these distant lands, but gained his expertise from books, maps, letters, accounts and through discussion with returning colleagues or colonists. William's deep enthusiasm for colonial opportunity found physical expression when it came to rebuilding Dyrham Park. Associates and agents in the Americas procured exotic timber to build his new house, and cases of seeds and saplings to stock the garden and park.

William was also Secretary at War, administering the army for a decade while it carried out campaigns in Flanders during the reign of William III. When the King was abroad, William became acting Secretary of State, a unique arrangement that gave him access to the most sensitive inside knowledge and made him a central conduit for all government communications. As if this was not enough for any career, William was also Clerk to the Privy Council (1678–1714), and an MP twice.

Active, present and efficient

What marks William out was not great political achievement or the wielding of power, but something more subtle: his personal aptitude and capacity for work enabled him to fulfil the demands of very different offices, mostly held at the same time, and to do so competently and over many years. William Blathwayt was active, present and efficient. Throughout a turbulent period in British history, his personal experience gave him a ringside seat on events of lasting significance.

Above right **Blathwayt shared Queen Mary's love of blue-and-white china; by studio of Willem Wissing, c.1685**

Formative years

William Blathwayt's father died before his first birthday, leaving the family in debt. William's maternal uncle Thomas Povey immediately stepped in and settled the estate. In future years, Thomas was to be enormously influential in William's life – setting his nephew on a career path into government and colonial administration and inspiring young William's cultural tastes and interests.

In 1665 William enrolled in the Middle Temple to pursue a career in the law. In doing so, he was following in the footsteps of his late father, but it soon turned out that this profession was not for him. Instead, in 1668, Thomas Povey negotiated for his young protégé to join the English embassy

in The Hague under its ambassador Sir William Temple, a highly cultured man. Perhaps Thomas had already spotted his nephew's raw ability and observed William's particular diligence and focus.

The embassy was a formative experience for William. The learned ambassador provided a lasting role model, notably passing on to William his great enthusiasm for garden design. In The Hague we can assume William first encountered the Prince of Orange; the future King William III dined regularly with Sir William Temple, apparently enjoying the plain English food served at the embassy.

William, who was still in his teens, used his time in the Netherlands for personal development. He and his uncle Thomas frequently corresponded about his educational progress and at times William evidently found his mentor demanding:

For Arithmetic I confess I have no more of it than will serve my turn at present, but that is so easy to be learnt that I will undertake in less than a month's time in England, to be sufficiently advanced in it. For the mathematics, sir, I assured you in several letters, that I had neither time nor convenience in this place to make any further step in it.

William learnt Dutch while at the embassy and so paved the way to making his particular combination of abilities indispensable to the future William III. Beyond scholastic tasks, his time in The Hague instilled in William an enthusiasm for Dutch taste which so influenced the house he created at Dyrham. Some of the items in the collection – such as the Delft plaques illustrating Chinese plants now in the Ante Hall – date to this early period in William's long career and may be mementoes of his stay in the Netherlands.

Left Sir William Temple; by Caspar Netscher, 1675 (National Portrait Gallery)

Right The Delft plaques, c.1670, based on illustrations of Chinese plants by Dutch traveller Johan Nieuhof

Thomas Povey

William Blathwayt would have achieved little without his charismatic uncle, Thomas Povey (c.1613–c.1705). Thomas was inquisitive, cultured, extravagant, socially adept and very well connected, although he could also be incompetent, especially in financial matters.

Thomas Povey also started out as a lawyer, entering Grey's Inn in 1633; he first came to wider attention in 1643 as the author of a pamphlet opposing the Civil War. However, Thomas proved he could roll with the times. Having narrowly avoided arrest in 1650, he soon became a leading colonial administrator, closely allied to the Lord Protector, Oliver Cromwell, and to prominent merchants.

After the Restoration, Povey retained his colonial influence, adding Treasurer of Tangier to his various other appointments in 1662. Within a few years, the accounts had become untidy, and Thomas transferred this particular role to his fellow committee member Samuel Pepys in exchange for an interest in the profits. Their relationship endured, Pepys often mentioning Thomas in his diary with a mixture of affection and derision.

'His company [is] most excellent in anything but business.'

7 September 1665
From the diary of Samuel Pepys

Right Thomas Povey;
by John Michael Wright,
c.1657

A man of learning

Thomas Povey was a founder member of the Royal Society – that great 'club' of England's leading intellectuals, philosophers and scientists formed in 1660. He helped find the Society a permanent venue and acquire its first scientific collections. Thomas chaired a committee responsible for sending letters all over the world requesting information and exotic specimens. Thomas nominated several of his friends to the Society, including Samuel Pepys, who went on to become president.

Thomas was also an enthusiastic collector, especially of paintings and books, which he sold to William Blathwayt in 1693; today these form the core of the Dyrham collection. Thomas owned the two important perspective paintings by Samuel van Hoogstraten; he knew the artist and entertained him to dinner. Pepys also dined at Thomas's house and described a lavish menu.

Indeed, a guest could even request a dish of their choice and it would instantly arrive at the table. Pepys also expressed particular interest in his illusionistic paintings by Hoogstraten.

During his lifetime, Thomas was a generous donor, giving rare books to the College of Arms, and paintings and ethnographic items to the Royal Society.

'I find him [Povey] a fine gentleman, and one that loves to live nobly and neatly, as I perceive by his discourse of his house, pictures, and horses.'

Samuel Pepys, 31 December 1662

Above **Samuel Pepys; by John Hayls, 1666 (National Portrait Gallery)**

Left **Detail of Hoogstraten's** *Perspective View of the Courtyard of a House*

A Mapp of Virginia,
Mary-Land, New-Jarsey,
New-York & New-England.
By John Thornton at the Sundyal
in the Minories and by
Robert Greene at ye Rose and
Crowne in Budgerow.
London.

A Scale of Thirty English Miles

the Great bay of Chesapeake.

The Colonies

William Blathwayt was described in his lifetime as 'better qualified than any body' in colonial matters. In an era without a defined government strategy, Blathwayt filled the void through knowledge, experience and influence.

An unrivalled knowledge

Blathwayt's colonial career started in 1675, when Thomas Povey arranged for him to become clerk to the newly established plantation office, known as the Lords of Trade and Plantations. He quickly rose in prominence and became secretary from 1679 until it was replaced by the Board of Trade, of which Blathwayt was a member until 1707. Blathwayt excelled in organising the complex and disorganised papers and accounts, and on the Treasury's recommendation, was appointed Surveyor and Auditor General of Plantation Revenues in 1680, a post he held until his death.

Blathwayt's career in colonial matters lasted over 40 years and from the start he attained an unrivalled knowledge in the subject. With knowledge came power. He promoted his allies, and was once described as 'always the patron of those who hold the Quill'. When colonists wanted jobs or needed assistance, they courted Blathwayt with cash gifts and occasionally more unusual treats such as gloves, beaver pelts or marmalade.

Enlarging the empire

Unsurprisingly, Blathwayt never spelled out his aims for the colonies, perhaps seeing no need for such analysis, and ever aware that his role was not to define but enact policy. However, he stated that the colonies 'enlarge the Empire and increase the revenues very considerably'. Historians argue Blathwayt consistently promoted imperial ambitions, encouraging well-disciplined colonies run by governors who exercised military control to maintain order and develop production and trade. Blathwayt described his own legacy: where once colonies were 'desperate ventures of little importance', they were now 'necessary and important members' of the realm. We can see Blathwayt present and active in the formation of a British idea of Empire, championing a course that defined the following centuries. This enthusiasm for colonial opportunity found physical expression at Dyrham Park. His closest colleagues and agents in the Americas procured exotic timber to build his new house, and cases of seeds and saplings to stock the garden and park.

The great survivor

By 1683, William Blathwayt was in a position to purchase the role of Secretary at War. This was a civilian post concerned with army recruitment, logistics and accommodation, and – the most important duty – arranging pay.

William knew nothing about military matters on his appointment, but he immediately wrote to the British envoy in France asking for useful books, possibly the same volumes surviving in the Dyrham collection to this day.

William's first tasks involved reorganisation, and perhaps he did not anticipate the job becoming such an eventful one. In 1688 everything changed. As a servant of the reigning monarch, William found himself bound to James II as

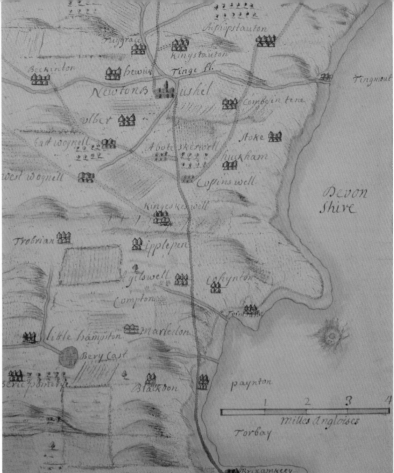

England prepared for an invasion by William, Prince of Orange. He loyally marched westward in the King's entourage, advancing towards the invading forces. When the royal party reached Salisbury, it was William Blathwayt who issued the fateful instructions that James, suffering from nosebleeds, should return to London. This proved to be a defining moment of the Glorious Revolution, sounding a retreat that within weeks resulted in James's flight and exile. Blathwayt, ever the professional, switched his allegiance to the new king and queen with minimal fuss. Just weeks after the coup and still fully 'in post', he was sharing instructions with his counterpart at the Admiralty, Samuel Pepys, and wishing him a happy Christmas.

Above Blathwayt's copy of a map, showing (in red) William of Orange's invasion route

Left William III in classical armour

An assiduous servant

Under William III, warfare was never far away. The army was first active in Ireland, resisting the deposed James II. Blathwayt flatly refused to attend in Ireland and even tendered his resignation. It was not accepted. Queen Mary was incredulous, writing to her husband, 'I wondered why you wou'd let him serve here, since he wou'd not go with you [to Ireland], but I said I supposed you knew why you did it'.

At war in Flanders

The reason for the King's trust in Blathwayt became apparent when the attention moved to Flanders and war against the French king, Louis XIV. As commander-in-chief, William needed a secretary at war, but had little desire to have more powerful secretaries of state in attendance. Their countersignatures were necessary for government procedure, but he was suspicious of their political weight and disliked any challenge to his trusted favourites. From 1692 the King solved the problem by conferring on Blathwayt the role of acting secretary of state when abroad. This suited the secretaries of state at home, who had no desire to go on lengthy and dangerous military campaigns. The advantage to the King was that he gained an assiduous servant who offered no opinion on political matters.

A decade spent on summer campaigning was not without risk. In 1694 a cannon ball killed the deputy director of the Bank of England, standing next to Blathwayt as they viewed a battlefield. But there were also opportunities: each period of seasonal warfare started and ended with time spent in The Hague and at the King's various hunting estates. Blathwayt had opportunities to stay in fashionable and luxurious houses, visit gardens and meet designers and artists. He bought books, paintings, textiles and Delft ceramics, all to furnish his new house then under construction at Dyrham.

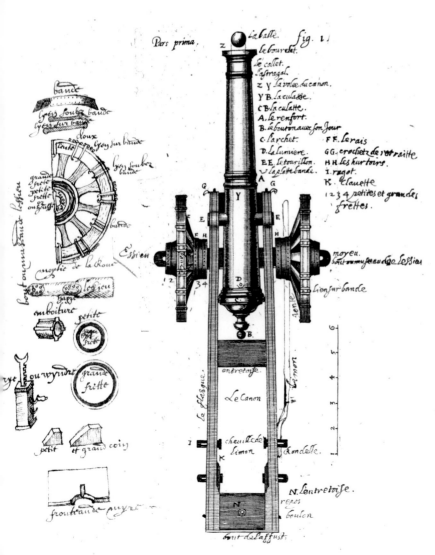

Making a dynasty

In 1686 William Blathwayt married the Dyrham heiress Mary Wynter. His career was in the ascendant, his income growing both officially and under the table, but he lacked the public signifiers for a man of wealth and status – a family and a country estate. Through Mary and her inheritance, he acquired both in quick succession.

The marriage was brokered by Thomas Povey's friend and William's mentor, Sir Robert Southwell of Kings Weston, Bristol. There were hard negotiations over the financial settlement, though William claimed he was more attracted to his

betrothed than to her estate. The Wynters were an established West Country family with a proud seafaring history; their ancestors had commanded ships at the time of the Spanish Armada.

The wedding took place on 23 December 1686 at Dyrham's parish church, next to the rambling and somewhat decrepit Wynter family home. Sir Robert Southwell attended and conveyed to the happy couple the best wishes of Samuel Pepys. We know little about their lives together, although we do know that they lived in London until Mary's father died and that they had two

Above Mary Wynter; by Michael Dahl, c.1689-91

Left Young William Blathwayt II; by Henry Tilson, 1691

sons, William and John, and a daughter, Anne. Mary Blathwayt died in November 1691, possibly from complications following childbirth. William never remarried. He never mentions his wife in his correspondence, and none of her letters survives. If it were not for Mary's portrait by Michael Dahl, we would have nothing to imagine her by.

A portrait of the Blathwayts' elder son William from 1691 depicts the three-year-old in classical dress with the military paraphernalia of drum, sword and spear. It captures his father's optimism in that year: his career was buoyant; he was established as Secretary at War, working ever more closely with the King; he was happily married with children, the owner of a large estate and planning work on a new house and gardens. Just months later, Mary died but, despite his loss, William's house, garden and career continued to blossom. An unmarried sister, Elisabeth Blathwayt, moved in to look after William's children but we know little about their early upbringing and education.

The next generation

The elder son, another William, married at the chapel of Gray's Inn in London, which suggests he studied the law there, but his life was, it seems, quiet and unremarkable and he simply fulfilled the role of country squire at Dyrham Park. His younger brother John had an altogether more interesting life. He became a colonel in the army, but, always musically gifted, he founded an opera company with Handel. Anne Blathwayt married Sir Robert Southwell's son, Edward, although she died within a year during childbirth.

Above **Anne Blathwayt**

Left **John Blathwayt; by Wilhelm Sonmans, 1702**

'I din'd at Mr Blathwayt's. This gentleman is Secretary of War, Clerk of the Counsel, etc., having raised himselfe by his industry from very moderate circumstances. He is a very proper handsome person, and very dextrous in buisinesse, and has besides all this, married a very great fortune.'

From the diary of John Evelyn, 18 June 1687

The Grand Tour

From the late sixteenth century, men of consequence went on a Grand Tour of continental Europe to conclude their education. What started as a rare practice became essential for ambitious families.

William Blathwayt had gone on a Grand Tour of sorts after his Dutch posting. Having returned to London from The Hague in January 1672, he managed to find a place on the diplomatic mission to Denmark under the Duke of Richmond. After a few weeks in Copenhagen William was sent to look after the British embassy in Stockholm and then on to various German cities via Poland. His duties seemed conspicuously light. In October he was tasked to find horses for the Duke in Leipzig, and by the end of the year he was in Venice. As he wrote home, he was enjoying the 'merry-making and preparing for their famous carnival'.

Two very different brothers

Blathwayt's continental tour must have left a lasting impression, as he diligently prepared his sons for a more expansive version of their own. In summer 1703 when young William was aged fifteen and John thirteen, they were sent on a trial run to the north of England under the care of their Huguenot (French Protestant) tutor, Monsieur de Blainville. The boys left London in

Left William Blathwayt II; painted in Rome by English artist Edward Gouge in 1707

May and travelled as far as Kendal via Cambridge, York and Newcastle. They took in great houses such as Audley End and Burghley and cathedrals including Lincoln and Durham.

In January 1705, William sent his sons on a greater adventure. Again under Blainville's tutelage, the boys travelled first to the Netherlands, meeting many of their father's old associates and perhaps seeing places they had heard him describe. They had to avoid France due to conflict, and passed into Germany travelling via Augsburg to Geneva where they spent some time with more of their father's friends. There they studied languages and mathematics, but also practiced riding and fencing. The all-important trip into Italy lasted over a year and encompassed an area from Venice to Naples, including Rome and Turin. They studied the classics, and visited ruins, churches and palazzi. John also met and played with many musicians. In 1709, the young Blathwayts returned, via Vienna, Prague and Berlin, to the Netherlands where their trip had started four years earlier.

'Up until now I have never observed a major fault nor inclination towards any debauchery; everything would go as well as possible, if the elder could pay a little more attention to what he is told, and if the younger could rid himself of the too high opinion he has of his attainments and his ability. But once more, I hope that before their return to England, with greater age and more experience that they will then have, these little shortcomings will have been cured.'

Letter to Blathwayt from M de Blainville, Augsburg, 6 January 1707

Above John Blathwayt; by Edward Gouge, 1707

Throughout their Grand Tour, their tutor Blainville corresponded with William, receiving his careful instructions over matters of itinerary, education and social engagements. It is clear that the elder son, William, struggled academically but John excelled, especially in music, his abilities causing quite a stir in the courts of Europe. Letters from Blainville report his charges' progress and paint a picture of two very different brothers.

The Wynters of Dyrham

Dyrham Park came into the possession of William Blathwayt through his wife Mary Wynter.

The house was Mary's ancestral home but was in poor condition by the time of their marriage in 1686. Still, the ancient estate and deer park had great appeal to a man rapidly growing in status and affluence. The same ambition may have brought Dyrham to the attention of George and William Wynter, two brothers of Lydney in Gloucestershire, who purchased the manor and park in 1571. They were wealthy naval administrators whose father had been a leading Bristol merchant, ship owner and naval treasurer for Henry VIII.

The Wynters were closely associated with Admiral Sir John Hawkins, a famous Elizabethan naval commander. They invested in his ships which during the 1560s made three voyages to the African coast to enslave captives. One of the foremost seamen of the sixteenth century, Admiral Hawkins was nonetheless considered the first Englishman to enter that miserable but undoubtedly profitable business.

Right The Dyrham estate map of 1689

A shared history

John Wynter's grandson was also named John and had been a noted Royalist during the Civil War. He suffered financial problems afterwards and his three sons and grandson predeceased him. Thus, his beleaguered estate became the inheritance of his sole surviving daughter, Mary.

Quite apart from the appeal and status of owning an estate, it is tempting to wonder if William Blathwayt reflected on the Wynter family's seafaring history. William's own grandfather Justinian Povey had been involved in early colonial enterprises at the start of the seventeenth century. Perhaps William saw his marriage as an opportunity to bring together two families which had promoted the nation's global ambitions over several generations.

Imperial ambitions

George Wynter also invested in maritime exploration, including Francis Drake's voyage around the world in 1577. His son John was vice-admiral on that expedition, although, in the event, he lost contact with Drake at the Straits of Magellan and returned home. He brought back captured Portuguese merchandise causing diplomatic tensions with Lisbon for Queen Elizabeth.

Black history
The 1575 Dyrham parish register includes the baptism of Gylman Ivie. How he came to Dyrham is unknown, but he is the earliest known person of African descent recorded in the Bristol area, demonstrating Dyrham's long association with the nation's global and colonial history.

Above **Admiral Sir John Hawkins** (National Portrait Gallery)

Right **Francis Drake. George Wynter invested in Drake's voyage round the world**

After William

After William Blathwayt, the story of Dyrham Park little troubles the local stage, let alone the national one.

Colonel George Blathwayt (1797–1871) fought at the battle of Waterloo in 1815, but no descendant of William had quite the impact of their ancestor.

A slow decline

William Blathwayt's elder son William inherited Dyrham, married a merchant's daughter, and is invisible to history outside Dyrham; even there he made few changes. The inventory drawn up on his death shows little difference from the house his father created, and visitors to Dyrham still delighted in the elaborate gardens.

Above William Blathwayt II as an adult; attributed to Enoch Seeman the Younger, c.1720-29

It was during the life of the first William's grandson that Dyrham Park began its long, slow but consistent decline. The prized picture collection was put up for sale in 1765, although many remain in the house, having been bought back by family members. The gardens were allowed to decay, and were finally swept away by the fourth William Blathwayt by 1800.

Saved by the Colonel

After a period of accelerated decline, Dyrham came to Colonel George Blathwayt in 1844. He inherited Dyrham through his father, who was half-brother to the fourth William; George (the Colonel) had only ever dined in the house twice before it became his, at the age of 47. However, he set about its repair and revival with sympathetic gusto. He took out a colossal £50,000 loan to buy the contents of the house which had not been included in his inheritance, and made substantial renovations to the roofs and kitchens. He also added modern conveniences such as heating and WCs.

The Colonel's improvements were of their period, but there is more than a hint of sensitivity for the seventeenth-century house. Indeed, some of the changes the Colonel made, such as repainting in the Balcony Room, were wrongly identified in modern times as original work.

An unkind century

The twentieth century was less kind to Dyrham. The Colonel's grandson Robert Wynter Blathwayt inherited late in life and was soon compelled to sell many of William Blathwayt's treasured possessions: the splendid State Bed, the majority of his library, one of the Pepysian book presses (see p.41), and a celebrated landscape painting by Meindert Hobbema, now in the Frick Collection in New York. In 1936, with clouds darkening over Europe, Robert died without a direct heir, and Dyrham passed to his late cousin's son.

Wartime tenancy

At first, trustees took over the management of Dyrham and found a tenant in Anne, Lady Islington, the widow of a local MP. The house was reorganised, boldly redecorated in pale colours, and new fireplaces and bathrooms introduced. It also hosted the Pro Patria Day Nursery evacuated from London to avoid the blitz.

In 1945 the tenancy was terminated, and Justin Blathwayt moved into Dyrham, but it was a brief revival, as the house and estate were prepared for sale. The Ministry of Works agreed to purchase Dyrham through the National Land Fund, an endowment to acquire places of national importance as a memorial to the war dead. The sale was completed in 1956, and urgent repair work ensued. Dyrham Park was first opened to the public in 1961.

Above Robert Wynter Blathwayt; by Francis Edward Crisp, 1911

Opposite Colonel George Blathwayt; by William Slater, 1850

Creating Dyrham

'I am afraid there will be a necessity of building a new house at Dirham or being at a very great expense in repairing this.'

William Blathwayt, 1686

After inheriting a rundown house in 1689, Mary and William Blathwayt wasted little time and in 1691 they started laying out new gardens in anticipation of remodelling the house. Within a few months workmen started demolition work. By 1694, a new west front had enclosed the original Great Hall, the historic core of old Dyrham. The Blathwayts' new apartments contained comfortable reception rooms at ground level, and bedrooms and nurseries for their children on the first floor. William's chosen architect was Samuel Hauduroy, who came from a family of architectural painters (see p.24).

Above The east front

The east front

In 1698, a second building phase started, this time under the control of a considerably more illustrious designer, William Talman, Comptroller of the Royal Works, and the designer of William III's new apartments at Hampton Court Palace.

First, stables and domestic offices were attached to the west front, as the remaining Tudor ranges were removed. The demolition was very slow, and it took until 1700 before work could begin on the east front. It was structurally complete by 1703, with the remaining interior decoration finished the following year.

Most building materials in the seventeenth century were sourced locally. Dyrham is unusual as William Blathwayt was able to use his extensive professional network to acquire building materials from across the world. English agents in Genoa supplied Carrara marble; those in Stockholm supplied deal (softwood such as pine); and contacts in the American colonies sent exotic black walnut and red cedar.

Nearer to home, the roof lead came from Bristol (probably mined in Somerset), while the roof slates came from Cornish quarries near to Blathwayt's mother and stepfather. The building stone came from quarries on the estate.

Top right The west front

Right A gilt leather panel installed in 1702

A shimmering jewel box

When it came to furnishing the house, William had experienced at first hand the very latest court styles and had access to royal and overseas suppliers. In October 1695 he imported a trunk of luxury products from the Netherlands. We only know about this because the English customs officials impounded it due to restrictions on fine goods. Blathwayt released his consignment when he proved the contents were for personal use; he was after all furnishing a new house. The trunk contained various Asian fabrics, printed silks and cottons with floral designs and exotic names: *Susses, Cuttanees,* and flowered *Pelongs.* There were also fine damask silks and crimson velvet fabrics. These bright and lustrous textiles must have beautifully offset the rich dark-panelled interiors.

Several rooms were hung with stamped leather panels, painted over silver leaf, to create a shimmering jewel-box effect; others had panelling painted to resemble different woods, such as cedar or walnut. The Balcony Room, immediately above the west front door, was decorated to resemble three different colours of marble. This passion for *trompe-l'oeil* paint effects reflected a contemporary enthusiasm for showing off artistic skill rather than any wish to save money.

Two architects

Two architects oversaw the transformation of the Tudor manor house into a baroque mansion. Their different social standing suggests William initially intended to keep costs under control, but soon succumbed to greater extravagance as his influence and income grew.

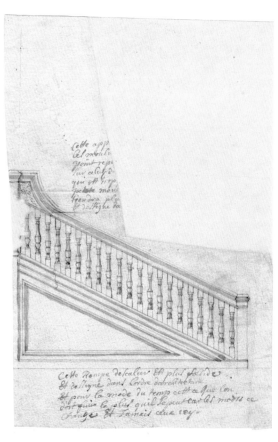

Samuel Hauduroy

Samuel Hauduroy designed the west front, built between 1692 and 1694. He is an elusive figure; we know his name, and a few of his letters survive in the Dyrham archive, but little more. He was evidently from an established family of decorative painters, who shared the distinctive Huguenot (French Protestant) surname. Better known are Louis and Mark Antony Hauduroy, who worked in the same period at the great house at Knole in Kent, and at Wrest Park in Bedfordshire. Hauduroy's designs cost Blathwayt the bargain fee of ten guineas. In a letter to Blathwayt's uncle Thomas Povey, Hauduroy complained that the cost of his carriage to and from London, including his food bill, had already cost him four guineas. Presumably, he stayed a while at Dyrham, as he grumbled at having to spend an age instructing and correcting the local workers.

A small number of Samuel Hauduroy's designs survive, including an early ground-floor plan and details for the Walnut Staircase. His client was involved in every design decision: one drawing has annotations in William's handwriting rejecting a baluster shape because 'this will harbour dust very much'.

A 'Mr Hauduroy' also painted the panelling in the new rooms. This could well be the same man or possibly another family member. The surviving bill provides a fascinating account of each room, the chosen colour or paint effect, with its cost per yard and the total length undertaken. By comparison with the fee paid for the architectural designs, the cost of decoration was over £185.

William Talman

William's choice of architect for the east front four years later was quite an elevation. He employed William Talman, Comptroller of the Royal Works, and effectively second-in-command to the surveyor-general, Sir Christopher Wren. Wren and Talman were rivals, but it was Talman who had recently won the contract to design the interiors at Hampton Court in 1699.

William appears first to have employed Talman in 1698 to advise on the construction of the Greenhouse and stables. Presumably at the same time William and Talman were planning the more significant project for the east front. Talman's London offices were in Scotland Yard, then part of the sprawling Palace of Whitehall, adjacent to the colonial office and across the road from William's London residence, Little Wallingford House. One can imagine the two men encountering each other as they hurried from meeting to meeting.

Talman certainly came to Dyrham on a number of occasions to check on progress, first in 1698 – when 'half a buck' from Dyrham's deer park was reserved for his visit – and again in 1701, when he was one of the very few people offered wine from William's cellar.

Talman is best known for his work at Chatsworth in Derbyshire, where he created what is considered the first truly baroque façade in England – the famous south front. However, Talman's interests were also in garden design; he worked closely with the gardener George London in all his projects, including at Dyrham.

Far left Samuel Hauduroy's early design for the Walnut Staircase

Left William Talman is seated on the left in this group portrait of the Talman family; painted by Giuseppe Grisoni about 1718 (National Portrait Gallery)

A very European building

William Blathwayt used his position as Secretary at War to acquire building materials for Dyrham. He asked his associates at various English consulates across Europe to find materials and arrange their shipping to London from where his deputies would send them on to Dyrham.

Italian marble

Sir Lambert Blackwell, the Envoy Extraordinary to the Grand Duchy of Tuscany, helped procure marble for the new house. William first wrote to him in February 1698 requesting six tons; rather

uncharacteristically he failed to mention what colour or grain he wanted. Blackwell assumed white, and it was duly ordered as five large blocks and 125 two-foot square paving stones. They were handled in Genoa by the British consul, who arranged for transportation on a military frigate. William wrote to Sir Lambert in the autumn very happy with his marble order though, as the letters were sent from the king's Dutch houses of Het Loo and Dieren, he had evidently not yet seen the delivery.

William was not just interested in marble blocks. He asked Sir Lambert to find him 'marble heads', which he had seen at Het Loo and wanted similar. He also asked him to find a sculptor for his own church monument at Dyrham. As William was organising this while on military campaign in Flanders, doubtless he was thinking of his own mortality. Sir Lambert found in Rome 'a great virtuoso about your tomb', but it cost too much; he then found a 'famous sculptor' from Carrara, who also made a design, but the cost was still beyond William's budget: 'their demanding being very extravagant'.

Norwegian wood

William called upon Dr John Robinson, the British envoy in Sweden, to obtain 'deal'. It is difficult to know what sort, as this is a generic term for coniferous softwood. Dr Robinson found a supplier of timber described as 'Norway', which may have been Norway spruce or silver fir. The consignment was shipped to London, where it was loaded onto another boat, bound for Bristol. This was the better

Left An unexecuted design for a doorway by Samuel Hauduroy

option, as another order bought in London and taken by barge along the Thames to Lechlade in Oxfordshire had cost £40 for the timber, but a substantial £10 for transportation.

Oak imported from Flanders was used to make the best doors, window shutters, and the new floor of the Great Hall. William could easily have acquired this timber in Britain, where it was readily available, but at four times the cost of domestic timber. Given that William spent his summers during the construction of Dyrham in Flanders, he may well have found a cheaper direct supply. Continental oak is quite different to our native species, which has a knottier structure and higher tannin content that tends to corrode ironwork. Flemish oak, often known as 'wainscot', came from straight, slow-grown trees, and was much lighter in weight and more even in colour. It was easier to work and did not damage hinges or locks.

Above The Great Hall floor was made from Flemish oak

Timber from America

Dyrham contains black walnut and red cedar from the North American colonies of Virginia and Carolina. These woods were used for the principal staircases and decorative panelling.

Once again, William turned to two of his close associates to find these desirable and decorative timbers. Edward Randolph was William's deputy surveyor and auditor-general, and Francis Nicholson was a lieutenant governor of Virginia and subsequently of Maryland. Randolph and Nicholson were also given the task of procuring American pine and cypress, used in the general construction of the house and for painted panelling.

Nicholson sent the first load of walnut in the summer of 1692. Randolph initially found walnut scarce in Virginia but sourced a thousand feet of it on the Potomac River. Pine was easier to come by: 10,000 feet of planks were ordered from a Quaker called Thomas Evernden at Little Annamesseck on the eastern shore of the Chesapeake Bay, today the town of Crisfield in Maryland. We even know the dimensions of the planks: 18 to 24 feet in length, over a foot wide.

Cedar used at Dyrham came from Carolina, where Randolph obtained five tons in 1694. The order was delayed while he made enquiries for a boat to take it up the coast to the James River; from here, it could be loaded onto a trans-Atlantic ship. Arranging shipping back to England was difficult. Quite often the ship's Master did not have the space to fit a full order, or would charge exorbitant rates. William criticised Randolph for not sending the walnut quickly, but as Randolph explained in his defence, a captain from Bristol 'refused to do it unless he were paid twice the value of it for freight'.

A mystery

It remains a mystery whether William Blathwayt actually paid for his imported exotic wood. There is no mention of money in any of the letters between him, Randolph or Nicholson. In December 1701, Francis Nicholson wrote to William from Virginia:

'I am very glad that the Cedar etc which I did my self the honor to send you, proved to your satisfaction, and have spoken to Colonel Quarry to wait upon you concerning some more, as likewise some black walnut for a summer house at ye end of your extraordinary Pile and noble upper Terras walk: and I am very ambitious of having the Stairs, wainscot etc sent you by him.'

Nicholson appears well informed on the construction at Dyrham, and he probably visited the house during his occasional returns to England. Presumably the timber was a gift for William, who wrote in May 1702 to say, 'I have almost finished my building… a parcel of good walnut will suffice if it can voyage by a Bristol ship'.

Left The first staircase Blathwayt built, as designed by Samuel Hauduroy, photographed in 1905

Opposite The Cedar Stairs today

Obsession from abroad

William Blathwayt took an interest in the smallest detail of his new house, even though he rarely visited during the period of its construction. As he was abroad attending William III in Flanders, he had to rely on his staff in London or at Dyrham to carry out his wishes.

William oversaw the construction by issuing written instructions, checking financial accounts and querying work programmes, all by letter. These have in large part survived and show an unrelenting demand for value for money, an obsessive control over the building programme and perhaps a rather impatient character. William developed a simple method to ensure his orders were clearly understood. He requested his cousin and agent Charles Watkins 'to write in large paper leaving a margin for ye answer'. William would then respond to each question on the original document and it was sent back to Dyrham. This flow of letters was critical for William, but always mindful of the costs, he was quick to spot where a saving could be made:

'Cozen Watkins, I have received yours of ye 8th which cost about 3s postage as exceeding two ounces weight whereas if you had sent your dispatch in two of more Packets, they would have gone free. Pray let this be a Rule to you and every body else for ye future.'

A major building project like Dyrham employed many trades: stone mason (opposite, far right), joiner (left), glazier (opposite right); prints by Jan Luyken, 1694

When his subordinates displayed a lack of resourcefulness – hardly surprising given his micro-managing – William was quick to bemoan their lack of initiative: 'I wonder very much this question should be asked me again and the thing not done before ye season passes. These questions are to be performed not asked.'

Clerks of works supervised the construction on a daily basis. First of these was the Dyrham rector, Samuel Trewman. He died suddenly in 1698, and was replaced by Arthur Wynter (presumably related to the late Mrs Blathwayt). He was in poor health and hesitant to accept the role, clearly aware that William was an exacting employer. The clerk of works in fact had little autonomy and answered to Charles Watkins, who managed the Dyrham estate despite living in Westminster. He seems to have shared the responsibilities with his brother, the two frequently paying bills, collecting orders and visiting Dyrham to check on progress.

William Blathwayt's most trusted associate was his colonial and Privy Council clerk John Povey, who acted on his behalf on nearly all matters professional and personal. Povey was a cousin and had married Blathwayt's half-sister Mary.

Finding and managing labour was a recurring challenge; in one instruction Blathwayt's agent warned: 'those kinds of fellows are addicted to laziness and ought constantly to be followed.' On another occasion it was discovered, '…a great part of ye Workmen have been Revelling and drunckening ever since till this Morning'.

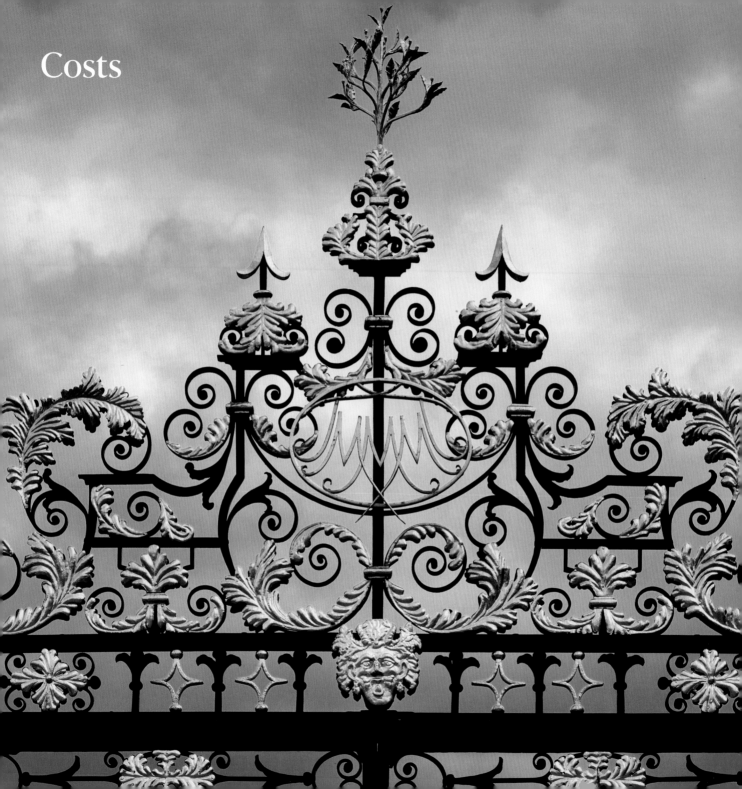

Costs

It is hard to know exactly how much Dyrham Park cost to build, as there was no main contract. However, the many letters, bills and receipts in the archives, and the gossip of rivals, suggest a total cost of around £15,000, well into the millions in today's money.

Driving a hard bargain

William paid for Dyrham from his income and not from borrowing, as was typical. The estate produced an income of about £1,000 a year, and William's salary during the 1690s was at least £4,000 annually. Gifts from many grateful beneficiaries of William's patronage and influence came on top. Perhaps Dyrham would have cost more if its owner had not driven such a hard bargain. He used a range of techniques to depress costs, including fining workers who were late or not pulling their weight, renegotiating a submitted bill and reducing the specification midway through work.

Dyrham's workforce

In the seventeenth century there was a general scarcity of skilled labour. This meant competition for the services of local workers, and difficulty in predicting their availability. Skilled tradesmen knew their economic worth, so if a better job came along, they were quick to abandon Dyrham, always to William's disgust. When local skilled labour was in short supply, expensive London tradesmen were found, but they required transport, board and lodging. Sometimes William despaired as labour costs

spiralled, believing his London joiner Alexander Hunter, 'intends never to have finished the work but to linger in the country at my expense'.

Most trades were responsible for supplying materials and labour. Bills surviving in the archives identify many of the men involved. Philip West won much of the masonry work, and later signed a contract with his employer to maintain the building. The plumber was John Avery from Bristol, who supplied all leadwork, from the roof to lining the plunge pool in William's 'bagnio' (like a Turkish bath). The celebrated Bristol blacksmith Simon Edney made gates and railings for the forecourts and gardens with wreathed pillars and brass ball finials. John Harvey of Bath carved most of the decorative stonework, including the Blathwayt eagle atop the east front.

However, the majority of workmen were unskilled locals, employed on an ad-hoc basis as directed by the clerk of works. Unlike today's building projects, there was no overall schedule. Instead, tasks were organised as they came up, with men employed often just for a few days at a time. During harvest unskilled labourers could easily get work in the fields and casual labour became scarce. William's technique was to pay by the day, but withhold full payment until the task was complete and so compel the men to return and work fast. It did sometimes backfire, when they simply refused to work for the fee on offer.

Opposite The Edney gates at Tredegar House, 1714

Left A carved stone swag on the east front

Bottom The carved stone eagle on the east front parapet

The Collection

The Dyrham Park collection, though not extensive today, contains examples of the items William Blathwayt assembled at the peak of his career. What we see today evokes something of the house he created despite the many losses and additions from later generations.

There are two detailed household inventories, one from 1703, as the house neared completion, and the second from 1710, as William entered retirement. They are broadly similar and the later one gives a full account of the house at the culmination of William's ambition. One striking observation is the sheer quantity of items: there were nearly 300 chairs, over 200 framed prints and more than 340 paintings. Principal rooms had vibrant wall hangings, and windows, doors and beds had curtains, some made from imported Indian fabrics.

There were many small tables in the house, often part of a 'triad' arrangement alongside tall candlestands and beneath mirrors to maximise candlelight. Some furniture was described as 'Japan', often an English attempt at oriental lacquer, although some items were the real thing. Fireplaces had grates or 'dogs' and equipment such as tongs and pokers, but fifteen rooms displayed luxurious Delft flowerpots in their hearths. Several of these survive to this day. They clearly demonstrate the Dutch influence in the furnishing of Dyrham, as do the gilt leather wall hangings and Dutch pictures.

What we have lost

Given the extensive quantity of material in William Blathwayt's Dyrham, it is clear much has now gone, including items that would fascinate us today. There were several birdcages, a large billiard table, two harpsichords, three globes and, rather surprisingly, only one clock. None of his sheet music or prints survive, nor any of the silver and only a tiny proportion of the ceramics. Gone too are the vast array of working items from the two kitchens, brewhouse, dairy and laundry.

Subsequent generations never comprehensively re-configured Dyrham; it seems to have slowly evolved with the times. The house was in poor condition and initially lost all its contents when Colonel George Blathwayt inherited in 1844, although at great financial cost he saved both structure and collection. The Colonel's additions include rich mahogany furniture, but he also introduced older, more delicate pieces, such as the painted

chairs by Gillows of Lancaster and mirrors by John Linnell of Berkeley Square. Both he inherited from another branch of the family.

When the Ministry of Works bought Dyrham, it acquired only a portion of the contents, enough to furnish the rooms earmarked for display. It was not the original intention to open every room to the public, but instead to lease out parts of the house as apartments to provide a source of income.

The selection of contents made in the early 1960s put the emphasis on the rarer seventeenth-century items, though allowed more expensive, plentiful or out-of-period items to escape. The National Trust has occasionally bought back pieces with clear provenance, notably pictures including a portrait of William III as a young man and most recently the bravura flowerpiece by Cornelis de Heem.

Opposite **The Ante Hall**

Above **The Diogenes Room**

Left **The painted Gillows chairs were inherited by Colonel Blathwayt from another branch of the family**

The great perspectives

The majority of Dyrham Park's paintings are those collected by William Blathwayt, including some purchased from his uncle Thomas Povey in 1693. They are but a small proportion of what was once a substantial collection.

The two paintings by Samuel van Hoogstraten (1627–78) are perhaps the most important works at Dyrham Park. The famous diarist Samuel Pepys mentions both several times. Thomas Povey purchased or commissioned them for his London home in Lincoln's Inn Fields.

A letter to Thomas Povey in *c.*1701 describes there being no place large enough at Dyrham for the huge *Perspective View of the Courtyard of a House* (*c.*1664) other than on the stairs. Here it remains in its original silvered frame (see p.9). *A View through a House* (1662) particularly intrigued Pepys, as it does visitors today. Hoogstraten captures that very briefest of moments – the split second after a door has opened, and the viewer first gazes into the world found within. The animals communicate this moment: the bird sitting ready to fly from the open cage door, the dog beginning a tentative tail wag. The black pillars frame the scene and support objects symbolic of women – the leaning broom and hanging key – that together

Right *A View through a House*; by Samuel van Hoogstraten (1662)

tell us this painting has a family story. There is a conversation happening at the table in the middle room. Two men face each other with a women sitting next to the window, in what may be a marriage negotiation. Does this women love the suitor? Who wrote the abandoned love letter on the stairs? Just visible through the side window is a man, his hand raised and about to knock upon the glass. Perhaps he has come to interrupt and declare his love?

Making chocolate

The artist of the unusual painting of a cocoa tree and roasting hut is unknown. Previous attributions have incorrectly suggested Albert Eckhout (*c*.1610–66), given he spent seven years in Brazil documenting the people, animals and plants. The painting illustrates the processes required to turn cacao into a consumable product: chocolate. There are fruit growing and ripening, and split open to show the seed structure. There is a container for the necessary pod fermentation, while the hut has drying racks to finish the beans for export. Blathwayt must have enjoyed drinking chocolate (at this date it was only ever drunk), as he owned chocolate pots and cups, and purchased from his uncle Povey the first book about chocolate by an Englishman – Henry Stubbe's *The Indian Nectar, or A Discourse concerning Chocolata* (1662).

'But above all things I do the most admire his piece of perspective especially, he opening me the closett door, and there I saw that there is nothing but only a plain picture hung upon the wall.'

From the diary of Samuel Pepys, 26 January 1663

Above **Detail of mid-seventeenth-century** *A Cocoa Tree and Roasting Hut*

Dutch
masters

William Blathwayt spent most of the 1690s serving William III in Flanders. When returning to England after each annual campaign, he had time to buy luxury goods, and especially paintings, from merchants in Antwerp, The Hague and Amsterdam.

Melchior de Hondecoeter (1639–1695) was court painter to William III, supplying works for his palaces in England and the Netherlands. William Blathwayt was an enthusiastic collector of his paintings, and no fewer than six survive at Dyrham today. Hondecoeter's fame stemmed from an unrivalled skill in depicting birds with ultra-realistic precision. William kept caged exotic and domestic songbirds in the house, which would have complemented these lifelike paintings. Moreover, he must have delighted in having so many pictures by his royal master's favourite artist.

William almost certainly bought the flowerpiece by Cornelis de Heem for Dyrham; the artist was working in both The Hague and Antwerp during the 1690s. Flower paintings served several purposes for their owners. They provided colour, life and obvious decorative appeal and were also pious reminders of the shortness of life. William would have certainly appreciated these attributes, but his greatest delight may have been in their highly naturalistic content. Perhaps such accuracy appealed to a man who built a successful career from his ability to remember factual detail across multiple subjects and all at the same time.

A Spanish connection
The painting by Bartolomé Esteban Murillo (1617–82) of *An Urchin mocking an Old Woman eating Migas* (c.1660–65) was in all probability acquired by William Blathwayt, possibly via his uncle Thomas Povey. This would make it one of the earliest works by this important Spanish artist to enter an English collection.

Murillo painted a series of scenes depicting street children, which were popular outside of Spain, and were in all likelihood directly commissioned for an export market in Antwerp. Both Thomas Povey and his nephew had contacts in Spain as well as in Antwerp where William purchased other paintings in 1693.

In the nineteenth century, another version of this painting entered the Dyrham collection. A family legend persisted for a long time that the copy was by Thomas Gainsborough, but analysis shows it is not by the famous portraitist, who only copied Murillo's religious paintings.

Remembering the place
William had a great love for topographical scenes, unsurprising given his colonial career and his extensive travelling in Europe. Some are of places he never visited, such as Tangier and La Rochelle, while others he knew, such as Portsmouth. But the years spent in the Netherlands, both as a young man and with the King, introduced him to many of the major towns. He collected their views, and there remain scenes of Antwerp, Delft, Rotterdam and Amsterdam in the Dyrham collection.

Above left *A peacock and pea-hen with a crane, flamingo, pelican and other fowl in a park;* by Melchior de Hondecoeter, c.1680

Above right *An Urchin mocking an Old Woman eating Migas;* by Murillo, c.1660–65

Opposite *A flowerpiece;* by Cornelis de Heem, c.1685

William's library

Books were perhaps the most essential items William Blathwayt owned; they were the repositories of the knowledge that was key to his career success.

William started purchasing books when stationed at the embassy in The Hague. Surviving letters show he travelled to Amsterdam to buy volumes on diverse subjects, including law, religion, geography and philosophy. He also bought books for friends and associates, learning quickly the long game of patronage and reciprocity.

One of William's strengths was his ease with foreign languages, most notably his fluency in Dutch, a very rare skill amongst his peers. An English–Dutch dictionary on the shelves at Dyrham (published in 1691) was probably purchased in readiness for campaigning in the Low Countries. He also had Bibles and secretarial aids in less common languages, such as Danish and Polish as well the more typical Latin, Italian, French and Spanish. They show William did not rely on any natural aptitude and invested time and money in furthering his skills.

The role of Secretary at War was not tactical; his duties were in communication, logistics, supplies and wage payments. Nevertheless, William took an interest in military matters. He had several books on campaign strategies including two versions of Jean Errard's volume on fortifications. One copy has handwritten notes and annotations, possibly by William Blathwayt himself.

In 1693, while construction of Dyrham was underway, Blathwayt bought Thomas Povey's library. This must have augmented an already sizable collection, and introduced many political pamphlets as well as books on the men's shared interest in geography and colonial matters.

Right Blathwayt's Dutch-English Dictionary. He was a fluent Dutch speaker

DE LA FAÇON DES BAT-
TERIES, ET DES EFFECTS D'ICELLES.

CHAPITRE II.

T d'autant que la force & violence d'vne mesme poudre est semblable & égale par tout en vn mesme Canon, il sera bon sçauoir quels sont les effects de plusieurs pieces ensemble, & de quelle façon on en vse pour les rendre plus grands.

L'experience faict cognoistre que les batteries qui se dressent de part & d'autre, d'vn angle en se croissants, (comme A & B, à l'entour de l'angle C D E) font bien vne plus grande ruyne, qu'vne batterie simplement de front; & semble que la raison soit, que celle-cy n'esbranle tousiours que d'vne mesme sorte : mais l'autre abat & renuerse, (principalement si les pieces sont tirées d'vn mesme temps, & à propos) comme nous voyons souuent plusieurs choses subsister, & demeurer debout, n'estans poussées ou esbranlées que d'vne sorte, & tomber facilement si elles sont en mesme temps chocquées diuersement.

Above Blathwayt's copy of Jean Errard's *Fortification demonstré* (Paris, 1619–22)

Right One of William Blathwayt's book presses was sold to the Victoria & Albert Museum in 1927

One notable volume is a French history with an inscription identifying William's maternal grandfather Justinian Povey as the owner. The gold tooling and initials IP on the cover suggest it was from Justinian that William inherited his bibliophile tendencies.

Luxury book cases

The several thousand books at Dyrham were predominantly shelved in William's library on the north side of the house, on the first floor. This tucked-away room, perhaps offering a cool and quiet spot for uninterrupted reading, contained two glazed book presses. One of the original pair remains in the house; the other was sold to the Victoria & Albert Museum in 1927 and replaced with a good copy. They bear a strong similarity to the set Samuel Pepys commissioned, which is now at Magdalene College, Cambridge. It is possible Povey's books came with their own luxury container, but they certainly demonstrate a deep respect for the careful ordering and keeping of books at Dyrham.

Furniture and furnishings

The furniture and furnishings at Dyrham, though limited in extent today, do contain important items from Blathwayt's original arrangement and give a vivid impression of the once luxurious home he created.

Few textiles remain in the house, given their susceptibility to changing tastes and the destructive effect of sunlight. Gone are the original vivid silks and Indian cottons that decorated walls and windows, but two sets of tapestries survive. The scenes of ancient philosophers in the so-called Diogenes Room are from Mortlake, London, and bills in the archive record their adjustment to fit the room in 1702.

Those in the Tapestry Bedchamber are extremely rare. Made in Lille, France, they show aspects of the famous gardens of Enghien near Brussels. William would have seen similar 'verdure' tapestries across the Netherlands and may have visited the actual gardens.

The State Bed

The most flamboyant item of furniture at Dyrham is the State Bed. The towering wooden frame is entirely covered in luxurious satin, silk and velvet, in a colour scheme of crimson and yellow. The designer is unknown, but it has similarities with beds by Daniel Marot, who worked for the royal household. The State Bed does not feature in the Dyrham inventory of 1703, and so the speculated date of construction is soon after, with a legend that William Blathwayt ordered the bed to encourage a visit by Queen Anne, when she came to Bath.

Symbols of slavery

The most emotive items of furniture are the stands in the form of chained African slaves. A letter to Thomas Povey describing developments at Dyrham specifically mentions 'the two black boys have a Proper Place on Each side of an Indian Tambour [tea-table] in one of the Best Rooms'. It seems likely the stands were formerly Thomas Povey's. Throughout his career Thomas promoted the colonies for their mercantile potential. He was associated with the Royal African Company – a group of merchant venturers who shifted their focus from West African gold and commodities into the increasingly lucrative slave trade – and perhaps saw these stands as signifiers of his expertise.

The 'Indian Tambour' in fact came from Java or possibly Vietnam, and probably arrived in Europe via the Dutch East India Company. The black wooden tray has gold decoration and legs of red lacquer. It was a special table for enjoying the equally novel tea, coffee or chocolate.

Together, these pieces of furniture encapsulate the reality of seventeenth-century England, for which trade had opened up as never before with commodities and exotica flowing into Britain from all over the world. The slave-figure stands are a reminder, however, of the human suffering that lay behind much of this explosion of prosperity.

Last of the leather panels
The Vestibule contains the remaining set of embossed leather panels decorated with putti, fruit and foliage. After more than 300 years, they are dulled by layers of varnish, masking their once colourful scenes, but the panels still have an iridescence from the underlying silver gilt.

William gave instructions to his workers to hang them on a damp day when the leather would be more malleable.

Left One of a pair of stands in the form of chained black slaves

Opposite The State Bed, *c*.1704

Delft

The collection of Delft ceramics is one of the most celebrated aspects of Dyrham Park; about a third of William Blathwayt's original collection survives, including some remarkably large items.

The Delftware, more than anything else at Dyrham, locates William's taste and ambition in the court style of joint monarchs William III and Mary II. For example, there are two pairs of extravagant tulip pyramids at Dyrham. These each have multiple-tiered nozzles to display the heads of seasonal, and preferably specimen or exotic flowers. They have the maker's mark '*AK*' for Adrianus Kocx, the owner of the principal pottery in Delft called '*De Grieksche A*' or the Greek A in English. This factory was the favoured supplier of Delftware to Queen Mary, providing her with many items but especially vases for displaying flowers. Her patronage encouraged courtiers to follow suit, but William had considerably better opportunity than most, given his frequent visits to the Netherlands, and consequently his collection became notable. The vases were used to fill empty fireplaces during the summer, replacing a dark void with colour, brilliance and fragrance.

Other Delft decorations included cups and ornaments, but also a pair of unique Delft tiles (*c*.1670) reproducing a published illustration of Chinese fruit trees. They come from Johan Nieuhof's book *An Embassy … from the East-India Company* (1665), which described the Chinese country, population and ecology – the result of the author's three-year posting. The imaginary

Chinese landscape, complete with various birds and animals, has three specimen plants in the foreground – banana, pineapple and palm tree, each identified in Nieuhof's book. The tiles would have appealed to William's strong interest in foreign peoples and geography, and his passion for exotic plants.

Superior planters

One of the most important plants in William's garden was the orange tree – a plant with deep and clear political meaning. The orange tree was not just a celebrated import, requiring the substantial investment of hothouses and knowledgeable staff for its successful cultivation. It was also a widely understood statement of affirmation and loyalty to England's Dutch king, William III, the Prince of Orange.

In 1696, William imported oranges and other citrus plants from a supplier near La Spezia in northern Italy. The delicate plants were personally escorted to London by a nurseryman who provided horticultural tips for the English gardeners. Once at Dyrham, the oranges over-wintered in the heated Greenhouse and then in the summer were placed out in the eastern 'best garden'. The plants were in whitewashed wooden tubs to aid their movement, but for important locations, they were placed in terracotta or fine Delft tubs. This was exactly how William would have seen orange trees at Het Loo, William III's most lavish Dutch house. One tub at Dyrham seems particularly pertinent for William, who surely would have been delighted by its design of deer in a landscape (see front cover).

Opposite Detail of a Delft pyramid vase

Below A group of Delft urns with William and Mary's initials

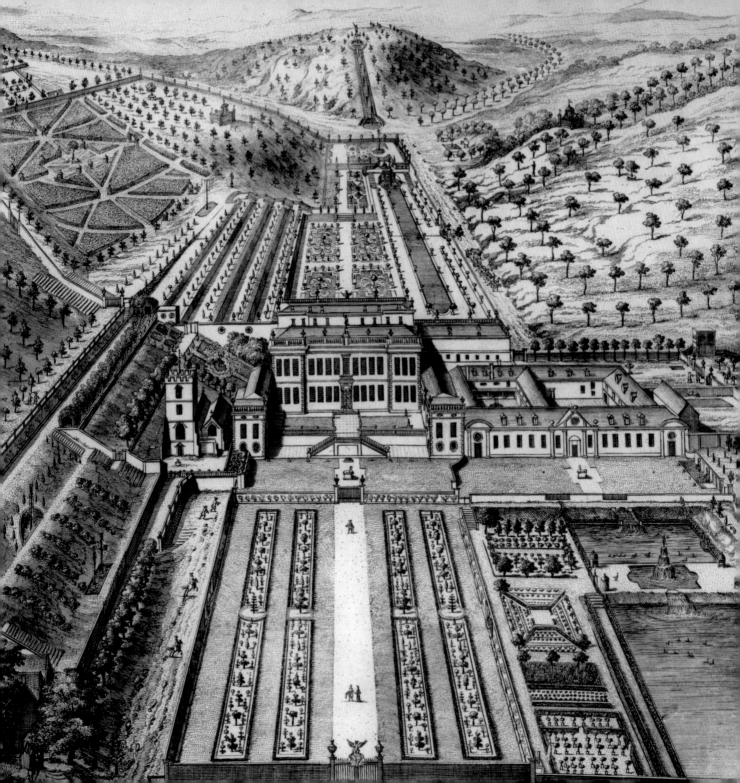

The Gardens

William Blathwayt created his celebrated gardens while constructing the new house. He consulted leading designers, but ultimately pursued his own ideas to create an ambitious garden that defied the challenging terrain.

In the age of William III and Mary II, gardens followed principles of interior design, marrying elaborate floral decorations with symmetrical, regular and formal layouts. William knew about contemporary gardens through books and prints, but he also had first-hand experience: because of his work, he was familiar with English royal gardens, and when attending the King abroad he took opportunities to visit gardens across the Netherlands.

The King and Queen were enthusiastic gardeners and their influence can be seen in Dyrham: the Queen was passionate about flowers, and the King delighted in formal design,

topiary and fountains. Courtiers, including William Blathwayt, followed this royal example and created their own magnificent gardens. William, of course, also used his colonial network to acquire a wide variety of exotic plants, and associates in the Americas sent large quantities of seeds and saplings.

Beyond the form and planting of gardens, seventeenth-century courtiers went further and introduced symbolic statuary and mottos into their gardens to demonstrate their commitment to their King and Queen; there is likewise a strong underlying expression of loyalty to William III at Dyrham.

Left Johannes Kip's bird's-eye view of Blathwayt's formal garden from the west in 1710

Right The west cascade today

'Most beautiful and delightful'

THE
Lover's Miscellany:
OR,
P O E M S
ON
Several Occasions,
AMOROUS and GALLANT.

In *Imitation of* Mr. PRIOR.

With an
Introductory POEM,
RURAL and POLITICAL:
AND
Mr. J. Philips's *Splendid Shilling* Imitated in Rhime.

In this Gay Age our Youths are Lovers all ;
But, tho' successful, they in Love must Fall.

L O N D O N:
Printed for J. ROBERTS, near the *Oxford-Arms*
in *Warwick-Lane.* MDCCXIX.

Above The title-page of *The Lover's Miscellany* (1719), which includes an ode on the gardens at Dyrham

Right The parterre at Hanbury Hall gives a good idea of what the Dyrham formal garden would have looked like in its heyday

The appealing engraving of the gardens and park at Dyrham by Johannes Kip shows William Blathwayt's creation at its peak in 1710. Kip is often criticised for elaborating his views of gardens to aggrandise and flatter their owners, but there is considerable evidence that his view of Dyrham was fundamentally truthful.

The view of the house and gardens was commissioned for publication in Sir Robert Atkyns's *Ancient and Present State of Gloucestershire* (1712), although it was paid for by William Blathwayt and cost £6 9s. The first account we have of the garden was before its completion. In around 1701 William's clerk of works, John Povey, wrote a description of all the key features: canal, cascade, parterre, terraces and fountains.

In 1718 Stephen Switzer published a long and detailed description of the gardens within his volume *Ichnographia Rustica*, one of the first theoretical considerations of English garden and landscape design. Switzer trained as an apprentice to George London and Henry Wise at their Brompton Park Nursery between 1697 and 1705, when he 'tasted… the meanest labours of the Scythe, Spade, and Wheel-barrow'. It is quite possible Switzer knew Dyrham's garden during its creation and once finished, as he worked on other local estates. His description of the garden is detailed, evocative and comprehensive.

In praise of the water-works

In 1719 Giles Jacob published *The Lover's Miscellany*, a selection of occasionally racy poems, but including an enthusiastic ode to the gardens – the water-works – at Dyrham. The author is more famous for his legal self-help guides, but knew Dyrham very well as he was William Blathwayt's steward and secretary between 1706 and 1711. His responsibilities included collecting rents, paying bills and organising repairs, and he used this knowledge subsequently to publish books on estate management, country sports, and parish and manorial law. Jacob credits his time at Dyrham as the source of his sound and reliable knowledge, though the claim that, 'I had many leisure hours, being fixed in a fine House with most beautiful and delightful gardens…' suggests William was uncharacteristically lenient towards his employee.

Extract from *On the Water-Works in Mr Blathwayt's Gardens at Dirham in Gloucestershire*

In Spacious Vale near to a Famous Town
A Garden lies, in Beauty yields to none;
A fine Canal runs through diverts the Eye:
Here large Jet D'Eau mounts Water to the Sky,
Around are Pipes in Multitudes discharg'd,
The Famous Works by Turn of Cock enlarg'd.
An Iris near adorns the Verdent Plain,
Produces quick a plenteous Show'r of Rain;
And Trees with Seats, which sprinkle oft the Fair,
Who thither for their Ease at length repair.
The Famous Cataract, my Muse attend,
Where Waves of Water in a Line descend;
From Step to Step they fall, and make their way,
And roar like Billows in a raging Sea:
High on the Top the pow'rful Neptune stands,
And with his Trident the Spring-Head commands….

The designers

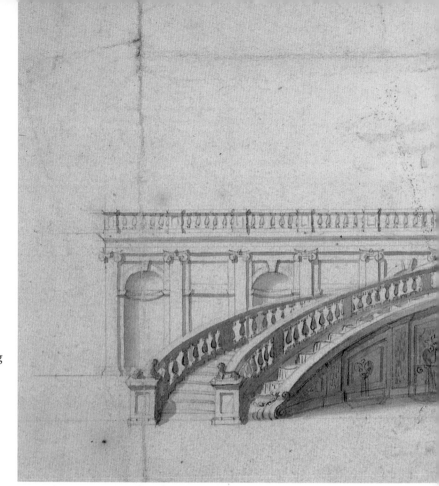

Several people were involved in the design of William Blathwayt's garden, all working at the same time and not really as a team. Perhaps the main creative force was William himself; in surviving letters he issued specific requirements, and though sometimes changing his mind, he took a close interest in the finest of details.

George London was the pre-eminent garden designer of his age. He was employed extensively across the country, possibly advising at over a hundred gardens from the 1680s until his death in 1714. London and his partner Henry Wise ran the Brompton Park Nursery, which supplied plants for these new gardens. London became deputy superintendent of the Royal Gardens in 1688, working extensively at Hampton Court Palace. Throughout his career London collaborated with architect William Talman, the pair ensuring houses and gardens complemented each other.

The first record of George London working at Dyrham is a letter from him to head gardener Thomas Hurnall in 1694 and he was still involved a decade later. Very few design drawings by London survive anywhere, but a plan of the eastern terraces in the Dyrham archive may be his. William once instructed Hurnall to thin a planting scheme, suggesting that 'Mr London is us'd to overstock his grounds'. Careful Mr Blathwayt was perhaps mindful that the copious quantities of plants proposed by his designer were to be supplied by London's own nursery.

It is not clear how involved William Talman was in the gardens at Dyrham Park, other than his established working partnership with George London. Talman designed the east front and its attached Greenhouse from 1698. He also designed an elaborate garden 'staircase'. Although this was never built, individual elements of the original design, feature throughout the gardens, especially niches and fountains.

Head gardener

Thomas Hurnall was head gardener at Dyrham Park from at least 1691 to 1710, throughout the design and creation of the garden. He probably left the same year William Blathwayt retired and moved permanently to Dyrham. Hurnall was highly involved in both the design and the planting, and in making plans for specific architectural and landscaping features. We know he travelled to nearby properties to collect seeds and saplings. Hurnall designed the fountain at the centre of the extraordinary 'slop't garden' and devised the heating system for the Greenhouse to support 'all our tender plants' over winter.

Leading sculptors

The gardens relied heavily on architectural form and ornament. William employed John Harvey of Bath, the leading local sculptor, who worked extensively at Longleat with George London. Harvey made a pair of large sphinxes for the western garden at Dyrham, numerous niches, fountains, cascades, basins and more.

Another important sculptor working at Dyrham was Claude David, an aristocratic Frenchman who practised in Italy before coming to England and working at Windsor Castle and St James's Palace. He made the surviving statue of Neptune, once part of a great fountain atop the famous cascade.

Above **William Talman's** drawing for the 'garden staircase' (not built)

Plants from near and far

Young plants and seeds arrived at Dyrham, bought from local suppliers, in London or sent by William Blathwayt's contacts in Italy and colonial America. The only plants surviving at Dyrham today from the seventeenth century are the veteran pear trees on the terraces.

Within the gardens, fruit trees predominated, grown in neat orchards or trained against walls. Most numerous were pear and apple, for eating and making perry and cider. Other fruits included crab apple, quince, cherry, apricot, peach and plum; these were kept as dwarf trees for easy maintenance and an ornamental look.

The most important fruits at Dyrham were the delicate citrus plants grown in the Greenhouse and moved outside in summer. In 1696 William ordered a large consignment from Italy. Giuseppe Croce of La Spezia escorted the precious cargo and met William in London to 'give you the necessare instructions about the planting and ordering said trees and greens'. The consignment contained citron (a type of lemon tree), sweet orange and possibly blood orange.

Right Etching of a Dutch orangery, 1685-95

William often wrote to his staff at Dyrham enquiring what was ready to eat. Records include carrot, onion, artichoke, savoy cabbage, cauliflower and pea. In 1696, 'a Gardener of Bath' supplied a thousand asparagus plants. A rich variety of herbs was grown, such as marjoram, sorrel and chervil, as well as those with medicinal uses, such as clary sage for eye problems and hyssop to relieve coughs.

The trees

Both deciduous and coniferous trees decorated the gardens and parkland. In the landscape native species predominated, such as horse chestnut, lime and elm, used to line the avenues. Ornamental coniferous species were used architecturally, to populate the wilderness garden; these included firs described then as silver, Norway and Scotch.

Shrubs and small trees provided structure and blocks of colour. Holly, laurel, juniper, pyracantha and phillyrea were bought in large quantities. Topiary took the form of pyramids, lollypops and sometimes complicated tiered shapes; it would have been grown from clipped dense evergreens, especially yew, bay and silver fir.

Colourful flowers

Little is known about the decorative plants that would have filled the flowerbeds. The Kip engraving shows fashionable widely spaced planting, and we know that flowers were grown for individual display and that perfect floral specimens were prized. Bright colours were popular and in the Dyrham archive there is reference to vivid yellow Spanish broom and red valerians. Pink was particularly favoured and present in thrift, rose mallow and sweet william.

Right A hunter's bag on a terrace; by Melchior d'Hondecoeter, c.1678. The orange tree alludes to the House of Orange

Exotics

A fascinating aspect of Dyrham's planting was William's unprecedented access to exotic species. His friend William Byrd of Westover, Virginia, a keen gardener, sent William a box containing peach stones, hickory nuts, tulip tree cones, black walnuts and cedar berries. Sir Edmund Andros, governor of Virginia, sent him a large consignment, which included myrtle, maple and red cherry, varieties of squash and gourd and *Magnolia virginiana* and yucca. Two plants sent to Dyrham were the first of their species to arrive in England: pink kalmia and white-flowering blackhaw viburnum.

Neatness and order

Looking after William Blathwayt's formal gardens was an unending and expensive enterprise. There were few permanent staff but casual labour was readily available to keep on top of its maintenance.

The impact of Dyrham's garden came through neatness and order. There were miles of masonry walls and gravel paths, and many painted timber structures that required continuous upkeep and were especially susceptible to weather damage. The intricate parterres, trained fruits, topiary and long flowerbeds all required routine care to keep them in shape and weed-free.

This great enterprise was managed by head gardener Thomas Hurnall, who at first earned £2 a year; his salary eventually grew to £30, which included board and lodging. From his office beneath the Greenhouse he had a bell 'to ring the workmen together in ye yard'. Casual labour was paid by the day, but work was sporadic and unreliable. Unskilled tasks were numerous, from carting manure to digging tree pits and paid around ten pence a day. 'Women weeders' could also find employment for only six pence a day and were often the wives and daughters of other labourers.

Various familiar pests plagued the gardens, in 1694 a mole catcher was employed and in 1696 'Paper & Powder & shott to kill Vermine' was recorded in the accounts. The same year, labourers John Perry and Joseph Smith provided 'wire Lettice to prevent ye Rabbetts coming down ye Stepps at both ends of ye Long Terras'.

Above Topiary cones were an important feature of William Blathwayt's garden

A gardener's library

William Blathwayt collected books on all his interests professional and personal. A few years after his death an inventory recorded all the books at Dyrham, and located several in Thomas Hurnall's office beneath the Greenhouse. There were many classic texts on horticulture, botany, garden design and technology. Isaac de Caus's manual on water-works (1659) provided an

essential tool for the creation and operation of fountains and cascades. There were general books of instruction, such as John Evelyn's translation of *The Complete Gardener* (1693), and what was probably a copy of *Den Nederlantsen Hovenier* (1669) – 'the Dutch Gardener' by King William III's head gardener. There were several books on plant care, notably on fruit trees, including *A Treatise of Cider* by John Worlidge (1676).

Brief glory

The gardens were a huge expense to maintain, and soon after their completion fashion started to move away from such formal schemes. By 1779 'the curious waterworks, which were made as a great expense, are much neglected and going to decay' and soon after in 1791 the garden ornaments once 'so numerous and sumptuous as to defy both Expense and Imitation' were 'now Reconciled to modern Taste'.

Right The title-page of *Den Nederlantsen Hovenier* (*The Dutch Gardener*), which was written by William III's head gardener

'Indeed, nothing can be more pleasant and agreeable, than a handsome Garden, rightly disposed, and well kept; no Prospect yields more Delight to the Eye, or gives greater satisfaction to Persons of a good Taste.'

From *The Theory and Practice of Gardening* by John James, 1712

Political gardening

HERCVLE

William Blathwayt shared a passion for gardens with his King and Queen, William III and Mary II. He did not simply follow royal example. Instead, he created ambitious gardens with an underlying message that clearly symbolised his loyalty and devotion to the Protestant monarchy.

Heroic Hercules

The orange tree is one of the most obvious statements of support for William III, the Prince of Orange. The fruit did not just bear the same name, but had deeper classical references to the legend of Hercules. The ancient hero famously performed twelve labours, the eleventh being to steal apples from a garden belonging to Hera, wife of Zeus. Hercules was successful, as he had courage and virtue. For William III's supporters the prince was the new Hercules, a courageous and virtuous hero for their cause and time. Consequently, William III's courtiers created gardens to display these fruit trees. A few, including William Blathwayt, went further and constructed ambitious heated greenhouses to cultivate these sensitive and prized plants.

The legend of Neptune and Aeneas

William III's heroism also found expression in the legend of Aeneas. The founder of the Roman people defended the city of Troy until forced to flee and sail away to modern Italy. In the legend, Neptune supported Aeneas by calming the seas. Allegorical links between Neptune, Aeneas and William III became very popular; one contemporary illustration even shows an Aeneas

with a distinctive nose rather similar to that of the King. William's invasion of Britain matched this classical story in the public mind: Neptune protected William (Aeneas) as he crossed the English Channel to land in Devon and start the Glorious Revolution. Poems were written about William's 'Court of Neptune', and gardens were frequently decorated with statues of the sea god. As at Dyrham Park, sculptures of Neptune featured in fountains, which apparently were the King's favourite garden feature.

The garden at Dyrham was an exercise in playing the political long game. William III wrote that his greatest passions were 'hunting and garden art', and so what his loyal administrator created at Dyrham seems to have anticipated a much looked-for royal visit. A motto written across the Greenhouse is a clear message to the King. It is a quote from the Roman poet Lucan: *Servare Modum, Finemque tueri, Naturamque sequi* ('preserve a sense of limit, stay on course towards a goal and follow nature'). The motto featured in a contemporary book on gardening and philosophy by William Blathwayt's first employer, Sir William Temple. By placing these words on the orange-nurturing Greenhouse, directly opposite the canal, fountains, cascade and ultimately the statue of Neptune, the garden's owner is paying homage to his hero, William III. The King would have understood the compliment and that the quote was borrowed by Temple, who was his close friend and favourite statesman.

Left **The Dyrham Orangery**

Right **Statue of Neptune, carved by the French sculptor Chevalier David**

Opposite **Hercules**

A place called Deorham

The deer-park at Dyrham dates from the early sixteenth century, but the roots of the name Dyrham suggest much more ancient beginnings. For William Blathwayt, a park was a signifier of status and its wildlife a valuable larder.

In 1511 Sir William Denys received a licence from Henry VIII to 'empark' 500 acres. In 1620 Sir George Wynter, Mary Blathwayt's grandfather, gained another licence, and after this date the park moved to the current location to the east of the house. On inheriting Dyrham, William Blathwayt commissioned an estate map in 1689 that shows the extent of the park including the rabbit warrens (see p.18). This would have been just before the new gardens emerged; as they took shape, so William bought more land and converted fields to expand the park.

The essential ingredient of any country house park is the deer, and these have an ancient association with Dyrham. The place name first recorded in the Anglo-Saxon Chronicle for AD 577 describes 'the place that is called *Deorham*'. The Saxon word deor means 'deer' and suggests these prized animals have been here for well over a thousand years. For William Blathwayt this ancestry was valuable, something his patron William III would appreciate should he achieve the honour of a royal visit and host the King's favourite activity of hunting.

Stocking the park was important and William received animals from the Duke of Beaufort's nearby Badminton estate. After the death of the King, friends enquired if William would host his new sovereign, Queen Anne. A visit was in truth never likely, and certainly never materialised, but perhaps more in hope than anticipation William once requested a young and particularly spotty fawn remain bottle-fed so the Queen might pet it.

A new landscape

The fourth William Blathwayt, William's great-grandson, inherited Dyrham in 1787; within a couple of years he had married and began a programme of expenditure. Local architect Charles Harcourt-Masters remodelled the gardens, and Humphry Repton visited and billed for his time, supplying a design for a summer-house. The neglected gardens were swept away. To the east a new entrance drive and lodges gave access to the Bath-Stroud road, and the approach to the house was re-landscaped to form the undulating parkland known today. To the west the garden was simplified. These works marked a divorce between the house and landscape, contradicting his great-grandfather's design intention that architecture, interior design and gardens were to be a single creative conception.

Dyrham's 272-acre parkland did not come with the house when it was purchased by the Ministry of Works in 1956, but through the Land Fund's successor, the National Heritage Memorial Fund, it was acquired in 1976.

Opposite **The Dyrham deer**

The deeper past

Dyrham Park is archaeologically rich, with evidence for human habitation stretching back to the Neolithic period. William Blathwayt could not have appreciated every detail, but a known historical past could only benefit his ambition to create a new dynasty.

The northern fringe of Dyrham's park overlooks Hinton Hill, an Iron Age hillfort, and the supposed site for the Battle of Dyrham. The Anglo-Saxon Chronicle records that in AD 577 Cuthwine and Ceawlin led West Saxons from the Thames Valley in a decisive battle against three British kings, Coinmail, Condidan and Farinmail. The West Saxons' victory secured Gloucester, Cirencester and Bath, but significantly, it pushed the British westward into Wales and Cornwall. It was perhaps one of the most significant battles on English soil.

Whether William Blathwayt knew of this event or its consequence is unknown, but it is possible, for in 1692 Edmund Gibson published the Anglo-Saxon Chronicle with a parallel translation in Latin. It would have been a volume that appealed to William's fascination for languages and history.

Within the park archaeological remains can be seen to this day. There are 'pillow mounds' for the rearing of rabbits, still very much in use in William Blathwayt's day. Ridge and furrow from medieval ploughing show where crops were grown, and that William absorbed agricultural land into his expanded park.

Above Footings for the sphix sculpture have been revealed through archaeological excavation

Left Cony catching. Rabbit warrens were still very much part of the landscape in William Blathwayt's time

Right This pendant was found in the garden in October 2015

William's lost gardens

Now also relegated to archaeology are fragments from William Blathwayt's elaborate seventeenth-century gardens. Excavations have revealed the footings for one of the sphinx sculptures that decorated the forecourts in the 'Western Garden'. Their receipt for £5 survives in the archives from sculptor John Harvey of Bath.

Further excavations by the upper pond, in the Western Garden, revealed foundations for the small pavilions shown in the Kip engraving (see p.46). The Best Garden to the east of the house, once resplendent with parterres, canal and cascade, has nothing above ground, but parch marks during hot summers show that much still remains below the surface.

The Tudor hall

There are many features at Dyrham we would now consider archaeological, though they were not so for William. His house replaced an earlier Tudor structure, and there are still some elements from the previous building. Perhaps most substantial is the Great Hall that survives in plan form, though how much original fabric remains within its walls is unknown. More obvious are the stone mullion-and-transom windows trapped in the basements, indicating the house was built on the older house's foundations.

Dyrham Revived

After a 'desperate illness', William Blathwayt was buried in the parish church on 30 August 1717.

He had already contracted John Harvey of Bath to sculpt his monument, but it never materialised, and his burial in the vaults remains unmarked. William's true memorial is Dyrham Park.

His life and career were not heroic, but they offer a unique perspective on a fascinating period of history – one that created the foundations of the British Empire and the beginnings of a global economy that turned London into a powerhouse of international trade and finance. Through his experience, we have an insight into the religious and political tensions in Europe at the end of the seventeenth century. All these aspects of William's life are reflected in Dyrham Park and help our understanding of this special place.

The National Trust is embarking on a period of renewal at Dyrham Park. Work started first in the gardens, and continues to develop features which reflect the extravagant designs so beloved by William Blathwayt. With the security of a new roof, replaced in 2015, attention now turns to the house interiors. Poor-quality modern paint schemes and gloomy interiors shall go; instead, we will reveal the significance and beauty of the interiors through redecoration and evolving displays. Above all, we can start to tell richer stories and share new ideas that will continue Dyrham's enduring relationship with the wider world.

Right The roof was protected by massive scaffolding during the repair project

Left The replanted beds in the garden

Family tree

Owners of Dyrham in **bold**
*indicates a portrait in the house,
including miniatures

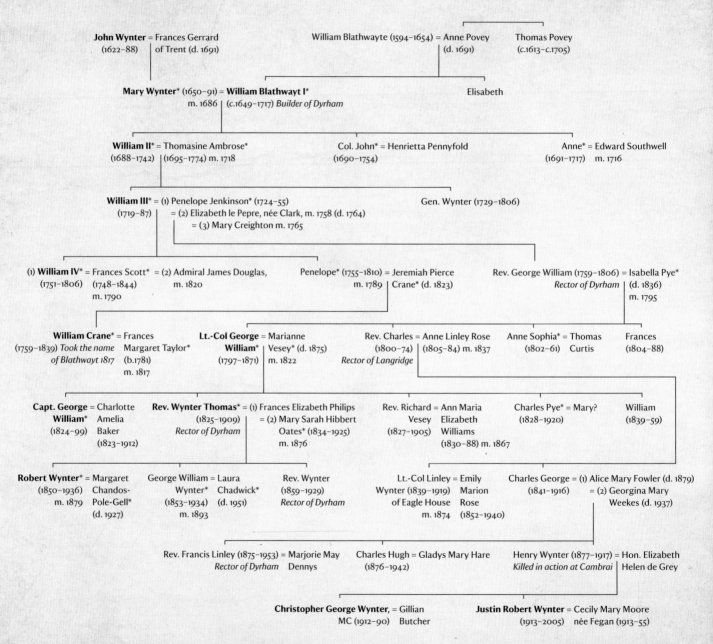

John Wynter = Frances Gerrard
(1622–88) │ of Trent (d. 1691)

William Blathwayte (1594–1654) = Anne Povey   Thomas Povey
(d. 1691)   (c.1613–c.1705)

Mary Wynter* (1650–91) = **William Blathwayt I***
m. 1686 │ (c.1649–1717) *Builder of Dyrham*

Elisabeth

William II* = Thomasine Ambrose*
(1688–1742) │ (1695–1774) m. 1718

Col. John* = Henrietta Pennyfold
(1690–1754)

Anne* = Edward Southwell
(1691–1717)   m. 1716

William III* = (1) Penelope Jenkinson* (1724–55)
(1719–87) │ = (2) Elizabeth le Pepre, née Clark, m. 1758 (d. 1764)
= (3) Mary Creighton m. 1765

Gen. Wynter (1729–1806)

(1) **William IV*** = Frances Scott* = (2) Admiral James Douglas,
(1751–1806)   (1748–1844)   m. 1820
m. 1790

Penelope* (1755–1810) = Jeremiah Pierce
m. 1789 │ Crane* (d. 1823)

Rev. George William (1759–1806) = Isabella Pye*
Rector of Dyrham │ (d. 1836)
m. 1795

William Crane* = Frances
(1759–1839) *Took the name*   Margaret Taylor*
of Blathwayt 1817   (b.1781)
m. 1817

Lt.-Col George = Marianne
William* │ Vesey* (d. 1875)
(1797–1871) │ m. 1822

Rev. Charles = Anne Linley Rose
(1800–74) │ (1805–84) m. 1837
Rector of Langridge

Anne Sophia* = Thomas
(1802–61)   Curtis

Frances
(1804–88)

Capt. George = Charlotte
William*   Amelia
(1824–99)   Baker
(1823–1912)

Rev. Wynter Thomas* = (1) Frances Elizabeth Philips
(1825–1909) │ = (2) Mary Sarah Hibbert
Rector of Dyrham   Oates* (1834–1925)
m. 1876

Rev. Richard = Ann Maria
Vesey   Elizabeth
(1827–1905)   Williams
(1830–88) m. 1867

Charles Pye* = Mary?
(1828–1920)

William
(1839–59)

Robert Wynter* = Margaret
(1850–1936)   Chandos-
m. 1879   Pole-Gell*
(d. 1927)

George William = Laura
Wynter*   Chadwick*
(1853–1934)   (d. 1951)
m. 1893

Rev. Wynter
(1859–1929)
Rector of Dyrham

Lt.-Col Linley = Emily
Wynter (1839–1919)   Marion
of Eagle House   Rose
m. 1874   (1852–1940)

Charles George = (1) Alice Mary Fowler (d. 1879)
(1841–1916) │ = (2) Georgina Mary
Weekes (d. 1937)

Rev. Francis Linley (1875–1953) = Marjorie May
Rector of Dyrham   Dennys

Charles Hugh = Gladys Mary Hare
(1876–1942)

Henry Wynter (1877–1917) = Hon. Elizabeth
Killed in action at Cambrai │ Helen de Grey

Christopher George Wynter, = Gillian
MC (1912–90)   Butcher

Justin Robert Wynter = Cecily Mary Moore
(1913–2005)   née Fegan (1913–55)